Delicious Sandwich Recipes

50 Easy-to-Make Ideas for Planning Healthy and Flavorful Low Fat Meals

Eddy Morales

Additionally, the information in the following pages is intended only for informational purposes, should thus be thought of as universal. As befitting its nature, it is presented without assurance regarding its prolonged validity or interim quality. Trademarks that are mentioned are done without written consent and can in no way be considered an endorsement from the trademark holder.

Table of Contents

ABC Sandwich

Ingredients:

- ❖ 1 cup mayonnaise
- ❖ 1/2 cup minced scallions
- ❖ 2 tablespoons brandy
- ❖ 1/4 teaspoon coarsely-ground black pepper
- ❖ 18 slices toasted whole-wheat bread
- ❖ Leaf lettuce
- ❖ 12 ounces crabmeat, picked over well to remove any shells
- ❖ Tomato slices
- ❖ 12 slices slab bacon, cut in half, cooked crisp and drained
- ❖ 2 avocados, sliced

Preparation:

In a small bowl, combine the mayonnaise, scallion and brandy, mixing well.

For each sandwich, spread three pieces of bread with a portion of the mayonnaise mixture.

Cover the first slice of bread with lettuce leaves, 2 ounces of crabmeat, and one or two tomato slices.

Add the second slice of bread, and top with the four half-slices of bacon, a layer of avocado slices, another tomato slice or two, and more lettuce.

Cover with the third slice of bread, secure the sandwich with wooden picks, if you like, and slice it in half. Serve the sandwiches immediately.

Acapulco Fish burgers

Ingredients:

- ❖ 1 pound fish fillets
- ❖ 1 medium green bell pepper, chopped
- ❖ 3 medium onions, chopped
- ❖ 2 cups soft bread crumbs
- ❖ 3/4 teaspoon salt
- ❖ 1/4 teaspoon pepper
- ❖ 3 tablespoons shortening

Preparation:

Bone fish; put through food chopper or chop finely with knife.

Combine with green pepper, onions, breadcrumbs, salt and pepper; mix well.

Shape into 8 patties about 4 inches in diameter. Brown on both sides in shortening in skillet over moderate heat for 10 to 15 minutes.

Alaska Salmon Salad Sandwich

Ingredients:

- ❖ 15 1/2 ounces canned Alaska salmon
- ❖ 1/3 cup plain nonfat yogurt
- ❖ 1/3 cup chopped green onions
- ❖ 1/3 cup chopped celery
- ❖ 1 tablespoon lemon juice
- ❖ Black pepper, to taste
- ❖ 12 slices bread

Preparation:

Drain and flake salmon. Stir in remaining ingredients except pepper and bread.

Season with pepper to taste. Spread salmon mixture on half of bread slices; top with remaining bread.

Cut sandwiches into halves or quarters.

Makes 6 sandwiches.

Asian Turkey Burgers

Ingredients:

- ❖ 1 pound ground turkey
- ❖ 1 1/3 cups canned French fried onions, divided
- ❖ 1 egg
- ❖ 1/2 cup finely chopped water chestnuts
- ❖ 1/4 cup dry breadcrumbs
- ❖ 3 tablespoons teriyaki sauce
- ❖ 1 tablespoon Frank's RedHot sauce
- ❖ 2 teaspoons grated fresh ginger
- ❖ 4 sandwich buns
- ❖ Shredded lettuce

Preparation:

Combine turkey, 1 cup French fried onions, egg, water chestnuts, breadcrumbs, teriyaki sauce, hot sauce and ginger. Shape into 4 patties.

Broil about 6 inches from heat or grill over medium heat 10 minutes or until no longer pink in center, turning once.

Serve on buns, topped with remaining 1/3 cup French fried onions and lettuce.

Yield: 4 burgers

Avocado and Chicken Tortas

Ingredients:

- ❖ 1 fully ripened Mexican avocado
- ❖ 2 (6-inch) sandwich rolls (such as Portuguese or submarine rolls), halved
- ❖ Salt and freshly ground black pepper, to taste
- ❖ 8 ounces grilled chicken breast, sliced
- ❖ 1 cup shredded iceberg or romaine lettuce
- ❖ 1 tomato, sliced
- ❖ 2/3 cup mashed black beans, divided
- ❖ 1/4 cup pickled jalapeño pepper slices

Preparation:

Cut lengthwise around middle of avocado; twist avocado to separate halves; strike pit with a knife blade to remove; scoop out pulp with a spoon. In a small bowl, mash avocado.

To assemble tortas: Spread mashed avocado on cut sides of rolls, dividing evenly. Sprinkle with salt and pepper.

On bottom halves, layer sliced chicken, lettuce, tomato, black beans, and jalapeño pepper slices.

Firmly press tops of rolls on tortas.

Yield: 2 sandwiches.

Avocado Bacon Sandwiches

Ingredients:

- ❖ 1/4 pound bacon slices, chopped
- ❖ 1 ripe avocado
- ❖ 1/2 teaspoon lemon juice
- ❖ Salt and pepper, to taste
- ❖ 3 tablespoons butter, softened
- ❖ 4 large slices whole wheat bread

Preparation:

Lemon twist and parsley sprig, to garnish.

Fry bacon until crisp. Drain on paper towels.

Peel avocado, taking care not to remove bright green flesh just inside the skin.

Cut in half and remove seed. In a bowl, mash avocado, then stir in lemon juice, salt and pepper.

Butter two slices of bread. Spread avocado mixture on buttered sides of 2 bread slices.

Scatter bacon over avocado. Cover with remaining bread slices, buttered sides down, and press together.

Cut off bread crusts. Cut each sandwich into 4 triangles. Arrange on a serving plate, garnished with a lemon twist and parsley sprig.

Avocado Chicken Melt

Ingredients:

- ❖ 4 boneless skinless chicken breast halves
- ❖ 1/2 cup cornmeal
- ❖ 1 teaspoon garlic salt
- ❖ 2 tablespoons vegetable oil
- ❖ 1/2 firm ripe avocado, peeled and sliced thin, divided
- ❖ 1 cup shredded Monterey jack cheese
- ❖ 4 wheat bread slices, toasted
- ❖ 1/2 cup plain yogurt
- ❖ 1/4 cup chopped sweet red bell pepper

Preparation:

Rinse chicken with cold water and pat dry with paper towels. Place between two sheets of plastic wrap and pound to flatten to 1/4-inch thickness.

In resealable plastic bag, combine cornmeal and garlic salt. Add chicken; close bag and toss to coat well.

In large nonstick frying pan, heat oil. Cook chicken in hot oil for 2 minutes per side or until lightly browned.

Remove chicken from pan, place in shallow baking pan.

Place half of avocado slices over chicken and sprinkle evenly with shredded cheese.

Bake at 350 degrees F for 15 minutes or until chicken is done and cheese is melted.

Place each chicken breast on a slice of toast.

Top with remaining avocado slices.

In small bowl, combine yogurt and pepper; serve with chicken.

Yields 4 servings.

Avocado Monte Cristo

A signature sandwich served west-coast style. Fresh avocados layered with turkey, Jalapeno Jack cheese, cilantro and salsa.

Serves 12

Ingredients:

- ❖ 3/4 cup garlic mayonnaise (aioli)
- ❖ 24 slices firm white sandwich bread
- ❖ 6 California avocados (3 pound)
- ❖ 48 (1 ounce) slices sliced roasted chicken or turkey (3 pound)
- ❖ 24 (1 ounce) slices sliced Jalapeno Jack cheese
- ❖ 16 eggs, beaten
- ❖ 1 teaspoon salt
- ❖ Unsalted butter, as needed
- ❖ 3 cups fresh fruit salsa of choice
- ❖ 12 fresh cilantro sprigs

Preparation:

Spread 1/2 tablespoon garlic mayonnaise on one side of each slice of bread. Cover 12 slices of bread with avocado slices.

Top each with 2 slices of chicken or turkey and 1 slice cheese.

Cover each with remaining slice of bread, spread side down, diagonally cut each in half. Reserve.

Beat together egg, milk, and salt; reserve. Dip 2 halves of a sandwich in egg mixture, coating well.

Brown in hot butter, about 2 minutes per side.

Serve with 1/4 cup fresh fruit salsa.

Garnish with a cilantro sprig.

Avocado Quesadillas

Ingredients:

- ❖ 2 ripe tomatoes, seeded and diced
- ❖ 1 firm-ripe Haas avocado, peeled and diced
- ❖ 1 tablespoon chopped red onion
- ❖ 2 teaspoons fresh lemon juice
- ❖ 1/4 teaspoon Tabasco sauce
- ❖ 1/4 cup sour cream
- ❖ 3 tablespoons chopped fresh cilantro
- ❖ 4 (6- to 7-inch) flour tortillas
- ❖ 1/2 teaspoon vegetable oil
- ❖ 1 1/3 cups coarsely grated Monterey jack cheese
- ❖ Fresh cilantro sprigs (for garnish)

Preparation:

In a small bowl stir together tomatoes, avocado, onion, lemon juice and Tabasco sauce. Season with salt and pepper.

In another small bowl stir together sour cream and cilantro and salt and pepper to taste.

Preheat broiler. Put tortillas on a large baking sheet and brush tops with oil.

Broil tortillas on a rack set 2 to 4 inches from heat until pale golden. Turn tortillas and broil until other sides are pale golden.

Sprinkle tortillas evenly with cheese and broil until cheese is melted and bubbling.

Spread avocado mixture evenly over tortillas and top each with 1 of remaining tortillas, cheese side down, to make 2 quesadillas.

Transfer quesadillas to a cutting board and cut each into 4 wedges.

Top each wedge with a heaping teaspoon of sour cream mixture and garnish with cilantro sprigs.

Baked Beer Burgers

Ingredients:

- ❖ 2 pounds ground beef
- ❖ Pepper
- ❖ 1 tablespoon Tabasco sauce
- ❖ 1 garlic clove, crushed
- ❖ 1/3 cup chili sauce
- ❖ 1/2 envelope dry onion soup mix
- ❖ 1/2 cup beer, divided

Preparation:

Preheat oven to 400°F.

Combine meat, pepper, Tabasco sauce, garlic, chili sauce, dry onion soup mix and 1/4 cup of the beer.

Shape into 6 patties. Bake at 400 degrees F until brown, about 10 minutes.

Baked Cheese Sandwiches

Ingredients:

- ❖ 12 slices bread
- ❖ 6 slices American cheese
- ❖ Butter
- ❖ 4 eggs
- ❖ 1 1/2 cups milk

Preparation:

Cut off crusts and spread bread with butter. Place cheese between 2 slices.

Place sandwiches side by side in a 13 x 9-inch baking dish. Beat eggs with milk.

Pour over sandwiches and let stand for 1 hour or overnight. Bake 1/2 hour at 350 degrees F.

Serve with cream of mushroom soup slightly diluted with milk poured over the top and warmed.

Baked Crabmeat Sandwich

Ingredients:

- ❖ 12 slices thin bread, trimmed
- ❖ and buttered
- ❖ 1 cup (7 1/2 ounces) crabmeat
- ❖ 4 eggs, beaten
- ❖ 1/2 teaspoon salt
- ❖ 1/2 pound cheese, grated
- ❖ 3 cups milk
- ❖ 1/2 teaspoon curry powder

Preparation:

Place six slices bread, butter side up, in casserole. Spread crabmeat over; add 6 more slices bread, butter side up.

Sprinkle with grated cheese. Mix eggs, seasonings and milk together and pour carefully over bread. Cover and place in refrigerator several hours or overnight.

Bake 45 minutes at 325 degrees F. Serves 8 to 10.

Barbecue Burgers

Ingredients:

- ❖ 1/2 cup onion, chopped
- ❖ 2 tablespoons flour
- ❖ 1 tablespoon prepared mustard
- ❖ 1/4 teaspoon pepper
- ❖ 1 pound ground beef
- ❖ 6 tablespoons catsup
- ❖ 1/2 teaspoon salt
- ❖ 1 cup sour cream
- ❖ 8 hamburger buns

Preparation:

Brown onion and beef. Add flour, catsup, mustard, salt and pepper. Add sour cream.

Serve on lightly toasted hamburger buns.

Barbecue Frank burgers

Ingredients:

- ❖ 1 pound hot dogs
- ❖ 1 1/2 tablespoons Worcestershire sauce
- ❖ 1/4 cup vinegar
- ❖ 1 to 2 tablespoons granulated sugar
- ❖ 1/2 cup catsup
- ❖ 1/2 cup water
- ❖ 1/2 cup chopped onions
- ❖ 1/2 cup chopped green bell pepper
- ❖ Hot dog buns

Preparation:

In an oblong glass dish, place hot dogs. Combine remaining ingredients except buns.

Pour over hot dogs and bake at 350 degrees F for 1 hour. Serve in hot dog buns.

Variation: Use ground beef patties in place of hot dogs and serve on hamburger buns.

Barbecue Pork on Buns

Ingredients:

- ❖ 1 (2-pound) boneless pork loin
- ❖ 1 onion, chopped
- ❖ 3/4 cup cola carbonated beverage
- ❖ 3/4 cup barbecue sauce
- ❖ 8 sandwich buns

Preparation:

Combine all ingredients except buns in a 4-quart crockpot; cook, covered, on HIGH for 5 to 6 hours, until very tender.

Drain and slice or shred pork; serve on buns with additional barbecue sauce, if desired.

Serves 8.

Tip: Pork can be made 1 to 2 days ahead; refrigerate covered and reheat before serving.

Barbecue Quesadillas

Ingredients:

- ❖ 8 (10-inch) flour tortillas
- ❖ 12 ounces smoked or barbecued meat
- ❖ 2 cups shredded Cheddar cheese
- ❖ 1 cup sautéed red bell peppers, julienne
- ❖ 1 cup sautéed onions, julienne
- ❖ 1 cup sautéed sliced mushrooms
- ❖ Barbecue sauce

Preparation:

Sauté onions, peppers and mushrooms and place in bowl. Shred or chop your meat and coat lightly with barbecue sauce.

Preheat nonstick skillet on medium. Spray pan with Pam. Place on tortilla in pan and cover entire tortilla with layer of cheese.

Top cheese with smoked sauced meat, sautéed vegetables.

Cover everything with another tortilla. Spray top of the second tortilla with Pam and turn over after bottom is browned.

When the bottom of the second tortilla is browned, remove from pan and cut into wedges.

Repeat process until all tortillas are used. Serve on a large platter with salsa, sour cream, and guacamole.

Barbecued Brisket

Ingredients:

- ❖ 1 (4 to 5 pound) fresh beef brisket
- ❖ 1 (5 ounce) bottle Liquid Smoke
- ❖ 3 teaspoons garlic salt
- ❖ 2 teaspoons onion salt
- ❖ 2 teaspoons celery salt
- ❖ 1 (18 ounce) bottle barbecue sauce
- ❖ Heavy-duty aluminum foil

Preparation:

Line a 12 x 9-inch or larger baking dish with heavy-duty aluminum foil, allowing enough foil to cover meat.

Turn brisket fat-side down and pour entire bottle of Liquid Smoke over meat. Sprinkle the 3 salts over meat.

Turn brisket over (fat side on top) and seal with foil. Marinate overnight.

Next morning pour off marinade; bake in a 225-degree F oven for 5 hours. Let cool.

Pour off gravy and refrigerate until cold. Slice meat with meat slicer on a thin setting or use an electric knife.

Layer in casserole dish the brisket and barbecue sauce; repeat several times.

Cook an additional 30 to 45 minutes in a 300-degree F oven until warm. Yields 8 to 10 servings.

Barbecued Pork and Beef Sandwiches

Ingredients:

- ❖ In a crockpot, combine the following:
- ❖ 1 1/2 pounds lean stew beef
- ❖ 1 1/2 pounds lean pork cubes
- ❖ 1 cup finely chopped onion
- ❖ 2 cups finely chopped green bell pepper
- ❖ Combine the following ingredients:
- ❖ 1 (6 ounce) can tomato paste
- ❖ 1/2 cup brown sugar
- ❖ 1/4 cup cider vinegar
- ❖ 1 tablespoon chili powder
- ❖ 1 teaspoon salt
- ❖ 2 teaspoon Worcestershire sauce
- ❖ 1 teaspoon dry mustard

Preparation:

Blend all of these ingredients well and add to the crockpot. Stir into the meat, onion and pepper mixture.

Cover and cook on HIGH for 8 hours. Stir to shred meat before serving on buttered rolls or pita bread.

NOTE: If you do not have a crockpot, you can simmer this mixture on top of the stove. Use a very heavy Dutch oven with a tight-fitting lid.

This may also be served over rice rather than using rolls, if desired. Leftovers freeze great.

Barbecued Pork Sandwiches

Ingredients:

- ❖ 1 pork roast
- ❖ 2 cups catsup
- ❖ 1 cup vinegar
- ❖ 3 tablespoons Worcestershire sauce
- ❖ 1 tablespoon prepared mustard
- ❖ 1/2 tablespoon Tabasco sauce (or to taste)
- ❖ 4 tablespoons butter
- ❖ 1/2 cup brown sugar
- ❖ Buns

Preparation:

In stockpot, boil meat in water for 4 hours or until it is falling apart. Of course, one can always use leftover pork roast, but you will need a lot!!

Remove meat, cool, shred. Discard the liquid.

In same pot, add catsup, vinegar, Worcestershire sauce, mustard, Tabasco, butter and brown sugar.

Boil for 5 minutes, stirring.

Mix in the shredded pork and simmer for at least 30 minutes but longer is even better!!

Barbecued Slaw Burgers

Ingredients:

- ❖ 2 pounds ground beef
- ❖ 1 medium onion, diced
- ❖ 1 bottle barbecue sauce
- ❖ 1 sauce bottle water
- ❖ 5 to 6 tablespoons brown sugar
- ❖ Buns
- ❖ Cole slaw

Preparation:

Brown ground beef and onion in small amount of hot shortening.

Add barbecue sauce, water and brown sugar. Bring to boil; simmer for 2 hours.

Serve on buns with Cole slaw.

Yields 10 to 12 servings.

Barbecued Turkey on Focaccia

Ingredients:

- ❖ 4 pieces focaccia or thick-sliced,
- ❖ country-style rosemary bread
- ❖ 1/2 ripe avocado, mashed
- ❖ 1 teaspoon fresh lemon juice
- ❖ 1/4 teaspoon prepared horseradish
- ❖ 8 slices barbecued turkey breast
- ❖ 4 slices canned pineapple, drained
- ❖ 4 teaspoons honey mustard
- ❖ 1/4 cup shredded Swiss cheese
- ❖ Lightly toast bread.

Preparation:

In small bowl combine avocado, lemon juice and horseradish.

Divide into four portions and spread on bread. Top each sandwich with two slices of turkey and a pineapple slice.

Spread 1 teaspoon mustard over each sandwich.

Sprinkle 1 tablespoon cheese over each and place under broiler, cooking until cheese is melted and lightly browned. Serve warm.

BBQ Pork Sandwiches

Prepare slaw; let stand to allow flavors to blend. Make molasses marinade for pork, then broil.

Serves: 6 - Total Time: 25 to 30 minutes

Ingredients:

- ❖ 3 tablespoons light molasses
- ❖ 3 tablespoons catsup
- ❖ 1 tablespoon Worcestershire sauce
- ❖ 1 teaspoon minced, peeled fresh ginger
- ❖ 1/2 teaspoon grated lemon peel
- ❖ 1 garlic clove, crushed with garlic press
- ❖ 2 whole pork tenderloins (3/4 pound each)
- ❖ 12 small, soft dinner rolls

Preparation:

Preheat broiler if manufacturer directs. In a bowl, combine molasses, catsup, Worcestershire, ginger, lemon peel, and garlic, add pork, turning to coat.

Place pork on rack in broiling pan. Spoon any remaining molasses mixture over pork tenderloins.

With broiling pan 5 to 7 inches from source of heat, broil pork 15 to 20 minutes, turning pork once, until meat is browned on the outside and still slightly pink in center (internal temperature of tenderloins should be 160 degrees F on meat thermometer).

To serve, thinly slice pork. Serve on dinner rolls with any juices from broiling pan.

Beef Burgers

Ingredients:

- ❖ 1 pound ground beef
- ❖ 3 teaspoons catsup
- ❖ 2 teaspoons mustard
- ❖ 1 small onion, chopped
- ❖ 1 teaspoon salt
- ❖ 1/2 cup bread, broken into small pieces
- ❖ 1/4 cup milk
- ❖ 1 1/2 teaspoons Worcestershire sauce

Preparation:

Mix all ingredients together.

Broil in oven, or grill.

Beef Sandwiches

Ingredients:

- ❖ 1 tablespoon dried minced onion
- ❖ 2 teaspoons salt
- ❖ 2 teaspoons garlic powder
- ❖ 2 teaspoons dried oregano
- ❖ 1 teaspoon dried rosemary, crushed
- ❖ 1 teaspoon caraway seeds
- ❖ 1 teaspoon dried marjoram
- ❖ 1 teaspoon celery seed
- ❖ 1/4 teaspoon cayenne pepper
- ❖ 1 (4 to 4 1/2 pound) boneless chuck roast, halved
- ❖ 8 to 10 sandwich rolls, split

Preparation:

Combine seasonings; rub over roast. Place in a crockpot. Cover and cook on LOW for 6 to 8 hours or until meat is tender. Shred with a fork. Serve on rolls.

NOTE: No liquid is added to the crockpot because the moisture comes from the roast.

Beef Sandwiches with Onion Marmalade

Ingredients:

- ❖ 3/4 pound thinly sliced deli roast beef
- ❖ 1 cup white or yellow onion, chopped
- ❖ 1 cup purple onion, chopped
- ❖ 3 green onions, chopped
- ❖ 2 tablespoons oil
- ❖ 1/4 cup granulated sugar
- ❖ 2 tablespoons cider vinegar
- ❖ 1 teaspoon Worcestershire sauce
- ❖ 1/4 teaspoon salt
- ❖ 1/8 teaspoon pepper
- ❖ Dash ground gloves
- ❖ 4 French rolls (6-inches)
- ❖ 4 endive or lettuce leaves

Preparation:

To make Onion Marmalade, sauté onions in oil in a large saucepan over medium-low heat 1 hour or until very tender, stirring occasionally.

Stir in sugar, vinegar, Worcestershire, salt, pepper, and ground cloves. Cook over low heat, stirring occasionally 25-30 minutes or until liquid evaporates. Cool.

Refrigerate in a tightly covered container up to 1 week.

To assemble sandwiches, bring onion mixture to room temperature. Place endive or lettuce leaves on bottom halves of toasted rolls. Arrange beef over endive.

Spread onion mixture evenly over beef. Place top halves on rolls. Cut each sandwich in half.

Benedictine

Ingredients:

- ❖ 2 cucumbers, peeled
- ❖ 1 medium onion
- ❖ 1 pound cream cheese
- ❖ 2 to 3 drops green food coloring

Preparation:

Grate cucumber and onion (may use food processor) and drain well in a strainer, pressing down with spoon to remove all liquid. Discard liquid.

Add drained cucumbers and onion to cream cheese and mix well in food processor. Color with 2 to 3 drops green food coloring.

Use as a sandwich spread or as a dip. Benedictine may also be used to stuff cherry tomatoes for an hors d'oeuvre tray.

Yields 2 cups.

Bistro Beef Sandwich

Red wine and roasted red peppers take this steak sandwich to new heights.

Serves 4.

Ingredients:

- ❖ 1 pound beef round tip steak, 1/8 to 1/4-inch thick
- ❖ 2 cloves garlic, crushed
- ❖ 3 tablespoons lite soy sauce, divided
- ❖ 2 teaspoons olive oil
- ❖ 1 medium red onion, cut into thin wedges
- ❖ 1 1/2 cups sliced mushrooms
- ❖ 1 jar roasted red peppers, cut into strips
- ❖ 1/4 cup dry red wine
- ❖ 4 crusty rolls (6 inches each), split, toasted

Preparation:

Stack beef steaks cut lengthwise in half and then crosswise into 1-inch strips.

Heat large nonstick skillet over medium-high heat until hot. Stir-fry beef strips and garlic (half at a time) 1-2 minutes or until outside surface is no longer pink.

Remove from skillet and season with 2 tablespoons of the lite soy sauce and 1/8 teaspoon pepper.

In same skillet, heat oil over medium high until hot.

Add onion and stir-fry 5 minutes. Add mushrooms, continue cooking 2-3 minutes or until vegetables are tender.

Add red peppers, wine and remaining 1 tablespoon lite soy sauce. Bring to a boil and reduce heat.

Return beef to skillet and heat through.

Serve beef mixture in rolls.

Black Forest Beef Sandwiches

Ingredients:

- ❖ 3/4 cup applesauce
- ❖ 2 to 3 teaspoons prepared horseradish
- ❖ 2 tablespoons sliced green onions
- ❖ 1 pound flank steak
- ❖ 2 tablespoons butter or margarine
- ❖ 1/4 teaspoon salt
- ❖ 1/8 teaspoon pepper
- ❖ 4 slices lightly buttered rye bread toast
- ❖ 1 cup shredded lettuce
- ❖ Sliced red onions
- ❖ Watercress

Preparation:

In bowl combine applesauce, horseradish and sliced green onions; set aside.

Slice steak diagonally across the grain, 1/8-inch thick. *
In large skillet heat 1 tablespoon of the butter to sizzling.

Add half the beef and sprinkle with half the salt and pepper. Toss over high heat until lightly browned.

Remove and repeat with remaining butter, steak, salt and pepper.

For each serving: place a slice of toast on plate; cover with 1/4 cup of the lettuce and 1/4 of the beef slices. Serve the applesauce mixture on the side. Garnish with red onion rings and watercress.

* Partially freeze flank steak to make slicing easier.
Makes 4 servings.

Beef Burgers

Ingredients:

- ❖ 1 pound ground beef
- ❖ 3 teaspoons catsup
- ❖ 2 teaspoons mustard
- ❖ 1 small onion, chopped
- ❖ 1 teaspoon salt
- ❖ 1/2 cup bread, broken into small pieces
- ❖ 1/4 cup milk
- ❖ 1 1/2 teaspoons Worcestershire sauce

Preparation:

Mix all ingredients together. Broil in oven, or grill.

Bleu Cheeseburgers

Ingredients:

- ❖ 1/4 pound bleu cheese
- ❖ 3 pounds lean ground beef
- ❖ 1/2 cup minced fresh chives
- ❖ 1/4 teaspoon hot pepper sauce
- ❖ 1 teaspoon Worcestershire sauce
- ❖ 1 teaspoon coarsely ground black pepper
- ❖ 1 1/2 teaspoons salt
- ❖ 1 teaspoon dry mustard
- ❖ 12 hamburger buns

Preparation:

Crumble the blue cheese into a large mixing bowl, and then thoroughly combine with ground beef, chives, hot pepper sauce, Worcestershire sauce, black pepper, salt, and mustard. Cover and refrigerate for 2 hours.

Preheat an outdoor grill for high heat. Lightly press the meat into about 12 patties.

Cook on preheated grill until browned on both sides and to your desired doneness. Serve on hamburger buns.

Bourbon Franks

Ingredients:

- ❖ 1 cup bourbon
- ❖ 1/4 cup brown sugar, packed
- ❖ 2 teaspoons Worcestershire sauce
- ❖ 1 cup catsup
- ❖ 1 tablespoon minced onion
- ❖ 1/8 teaspoon hot pepper sauce
- ❖ 2 to 3 pounds frankfurters

Preparation:

Combine all ingredients and simmer for 1 hour.
Serve in hotdog buns.

Brats and Beer

Ingredients:

- ❖ 4 bratwurst
- ❖ 1 cup beer
- ❖ 1/2 cup water
- ❖ Dijon-style mustard
- ❖ Hot dog buns

Preparation:

Prepare grill to medium heat. Pierce bratwurst three times with a fork. Place brats into a skillet. Add the beer and water.

Cover and bring to a boil over high heat. Turn the temperature down and simmer Brats for 10 minutes. Remove from skillet.

Arrange the brats on an oiled, preheated grill. Grill for 5 to 6 minutes per side or browned.

Take some left-over beer and pour about 1/3 cup. Brush on Brats as they cook. Turn the brats only once.

Brats are cooked when they are no longer pink in the center. Remove from grill and place in hot dog buns.

Add mustard and enjoy.

Brats 'n' Beer

Ingredients:

- ❖ 1 (12 ounce) can or bottle beer (not dark)
- ❖ 4 bratwursts (about 1 pound)
- ❖ 1 sweet or Spanish onion, thinly sliced
- ❖ and separated into rings
- ❖ 1 tablespoon olive oil
- ❖ 1/4 teaspoon salt
- ❖ 1/4 teaspoon black pepper
- ❖ 4 hot dog buns

Preparation:

Prepare coals for direct grilling. Pour beer into heavy medium saucepan with ovenproof handle.
(If not ovenproof, wrap heavy-duty foil around handle.)

Place saucepan on grill. Pierce bratwurst with knife; add to beer.

Simmer, uncovered, over medium coals, 15 minutes, turning once.

Place onion rings on heavy-duty foil. Drizzle with oil; sprinkle with salt and pepper. Fold sides of foil over rings to enclose.

Place onion slices on grill. Grill, uncovered, 10 to 15 minutes or until onion slices are tender.

Transfer bratwurst to grill. Remove saucepan from grill; discard beer. Grill bratwurst, 10 minutes or until browned and cooked through, turning once.

Place bratwurst in rolls. Top each with onions. Garnish as desired.

Brew Burgers

Ingredients:

- Brew Sauce
- 1/4 cup Heinz 57 Sauce
- 1/4 cup beer
- In 1-cup glass measure, combine ingredients. Microwave on HIGH 1 to 1 1/2 minutes until
- bubbly; set aside.
- Burgers
- 1 1/2 pounds ground beef
- 1 large, sweet onion, 1/2-inch slices
- 4 slices Swiss cheese
- 4 crusty white or whole wheat rolls, split
- Lettuce

Preparation:

Shape ground beef into four 3/4-inch-thick patties. Place onion slices on grid over medium, ash covered coals.

Grill onions, uncovered, 5 minutes.

Add patties; continue to grill, uncovered, 1 to 15 minutes or until onions are tender and burger centers are no longer pink, turning occasionally.

Season burgers with salt after turning, if desired.

Approximately 2 minutes before burgers are done, brush generously with sauce mixture; top with cheese.

Line bottom half of each roll with lettuce. Top each with burger, grilled onion and sauce. Close Sandwiches.

Cajun Chicken Sandwich

Ingredients:

- ❖ 2 (6 ounce) boneless, skinless chicken
- ❖ breast halves, butterflied or pounded thin
- ❖ 3 tablespoons Cajun seasoning
- ❖ Butter
- ❖ 2 toasted buns, split

Preparation:

Preheat cast iron skillet over high heat on top of stove. Dredge chicken in Cajun seasoning. Place small amount of butter in skillet and place seasoned chicken breasts in skillet.

Cook until seasoning is black, then turn and cook until done. Serve on toasted bun with your favorite sandwich toppings.

Makes 2 sandwiches.

Calico Sandwiches

Ingredients:

- ❖ 6 English muffins
- ❖ 3 tablespoons margarine
- ❖ 1 (6 1/2 ounce) can tuna, drained
- ❖ 6 stuffed olives, chopped
- ❖ 2 hardboiled eggs, chopped
- ❖ 1/4 cup mayonnaise
- ❖ 1 celery stalk, chopped fine
- ❖ 1/8 cup pecan pieces

Preparation:

Slice English muffins lengthwise, toast, then butter.

Mix all ingredients and put between the muffins.

California Chicken Cobb Sandwich

Ingredients:

- ❖ Two small loaves French bread
- ❖ 3 skinless, boneless chicken breast, grilled
- ❖ 12 pieces bacon, fried crisp
- ❖ 1 avocado, peeled and seeded
- ❖ 12 small, crisp lettuce leaves
- ❖ Dressing
- ❖ 4 ounces cream cheese, softened
- ❖ 6 tablespoons mayonnaise
- ❖ 4 ounces gorgonzola or blue cheese, softened

Preparation:

Combine ingredients until mixed well.

To assemble sandwiches: Slice the bread into 24 thin slices; toast the bread lightly on both sides.

Spread the inside of each piece of bread with sandwich dressing.

Cut the grilled chicken breast into diagonal pieces to fit the small bread rounds.

Top 12 pieces of bread and dressing with chicken, bacon pieces, avocado slices and lettuce. Top with remaining bread that has been spread with dressing.

Serve at once or cover with clean, dry lettuce leaves to keep moist.

California Club Sandwich

Ingredients:

- ❖ 4 slices baked turkey breast
- ❖ 1 fresh tomato, sliced
- ❖ 4 slices crisp bacon
- ❖ 1/2 fresh avocado, sliced
- ❖ Alfalfa sprouts
- ❖ 3 slices whole wheat bread
- ❖ Miracle Whip

Preparation:

Toast bread; spread two bread slices with Miracle Whip.

On one slice, arrange tomato slices and bacon. Add another slice of bread.

Arrange avocado and alfalfa sprouts on bread. Add plain toasted slice of bread to top.

Camel Hump

Ingredients:

- ❖ 4 pita breads
- ❖ Sliced cooked ham
- ❖ Sliced salami
- ❖ 2 tomatoes, sliced
- ❖ 2 tablespoons feta cheese, crumbled
- ❖ 1 tablespoon chopped ripe olives
- ❖ Lettuce
- ❖ Dressing
- ❖ 1/4 cup Paul Masson® Rosé
- ❖ 2 tablespoons lemon juice
- ❖ 1/8 teaspoon oregano
- ❖ 1/8 teaspoon garlic salt
- ❖ 1/8 teaspoon turmeric
- ❖ 1/8 teaspoon pepper

Preparation:

Fill each pocket bread with sliced meats, tomatoes, cheese, olives and lettuce.

Combine dressing ingredients and spoon over each sandwich before serving. Makes 4 servings.

Candied Corned Beef Sandwiches

Ingredients:

- ❖ 1 (4 pound) corned beef brisket
- ❖ 20 black peppercorns
- ❖ 2 bay leaves
- ❖ 3 tablespoons packed brown sugar
- ❖ 1 1/2 tablespoons soy sauce
- ❖ 1 1/2 teaspoon dry mustard
- ❖ 1 teaspoon ground ginger
- ❖ 2 tablespoons tomato ketchup
- ❖ 1 teaspoon red pepper flakes
- ❖ 1 teaspoon molasses

Preparation:

Place brisket in a pot and cover with water. Add peppercorns and bay leaves and bring to a simmer.

Cook for 3 to 3 1/2 hours until fork tender. Set aside and make glaze. Glaze Drain corned beef and place on a foiled baking sheet. Preheat oven to 350 degrees F.

In a bowl, mix sugar, soy sauce, mustard, ginger, ketchup, pepper flakes and molasses.

Brush brisket with glaze. Bake for 15 to 20 minutes, re-glazing two times while baking. Refrigerate overnight and slice across the grain very thin for sandwiches.

Yield: 10 sandwiches

Carnitas

This is one thing you can do with extra pork roast. Serve with warmed flour tortillas, more lime juice and finely chopped avocado.

Ingredients:

- ❖ 2 to 3 cups cooked pork roast pieces
- ❖ At least 1/2 cup chopped scallions
- ❖ Juice of 1 Mexican lime
- ❖ 1 to 2 tablespoons chopped garlic
- ❖ Salt and pepper, to taste

Preparation:

Preheat oven to 400 degrees F. Combine all ingredients in a roasting pan coated with nonstick spray.

Roast for 20 to 30 minutes on highest rack in oven.

Then turn on broiler and broil about 5 minutes to desired shade of brown. Makes 4 to 6 servings.

Carnival Corn Dogs

Ingredients:

- ❖ 8 hot dogs
- ❖ 2 tablespoons cornmeal
- ❖ 1 tablespoon granulated sugar
- ❖ 1 cup pancake mix
- ❖ 2/3 cup water

Preparation:

Mix cornmeal, sugar, pancake mix and water.

Dip franks in batter, draining the excess over the bowl.

Fry in deep fat for 2 to 3 minutes at 375 degrees F.

Drain on paper towels.

Carolina Pulled Pork Sandwich

Ingredients:

- ❖ 1/4 cup butter
- ❖ 1 1/2 cups chopped onion
- ❖ 3 cloves garlic, chopped
- ❖ 1 tablespoon powdered mustard
- ❖ 1 tablespoon paprika
- ❖ 1 teaspoon ground cinnamon
- ❖ 1 teaspoon cayenne pepper
- ❖ 2 cups catsup
- ❖ 1/4 cup packed dark brown sugar
- ❖ 1/4 cup apple cider vinegar
- ❖ 2 cups water
- ❖ 1 teaspoon salt
- ❖ 1/2 teaspoon ground black pepper
- ❖ 1 tablespoon vegetable oil
- ❖ 1 whole (5 pound) Boston pork butt
- ❖ 12 soft hamburger buns

Preparation:

Melt butter in saucepan.

Add onion and garlic; cook until softened, 5 minutes. Add mustard, paprika, cumin and cayenne; cook 1 minute.

Add catsup, sugar, vinegar and water; simmer, covered, 30 minutes.

Uncover; simmer 30 minutes. Add salt and pepper.

This can be made two days ahead, then refrigerated, covered. Before using, simmer 3 minutes.

Preheat oven to 350 degrees F. Heat oil in large ovenproof Dutch oven; add pork; brown for 10 minutes.

Bake, uncovered for 30 minutes. Pour 1 cup of barbecue sauce over pork. Cover pot. Lower heat to 250 degrees F.

Bake 3 to 3 1/2 hours, basting meat occasionally, until a thermometer inserted in the middle of the roast registers 170 degrees F to 180 degrees F.

Let cool slightly. Trim off excess fat. Pull meat apart using two forks.

Mix pulled meat with remaining barbecue sauce in a large bowl. Serve on buns with Cole slaw.

Cheese Sandwiches

Ingredients:

- ❖ 1 jar Old English cheese spread
- ❖ 1/2 cup (1 stick) margarine
- ❖ 1 clove garlic, crushed

Preparation:

Mix well. Cut crusts from bread. Cut into halves or fourths. Cover top and sides with cheese spread. Bake 15 minutes at 350 degrees F. These freeze well.

Cheesesteak Pockets

Ingredients:

- ❖ 1 tablespoon vegetable oil
- ❖ 1 medium onion, sliced
- ❖ 1 (14 ounce) package frozen beef or chicken sandwich steaks,
- ❖ separated into 8 portions
- ❖ 1 can Campbell's Cheddar Cheese Soup
- ❖ 1 (4 1/2 ounce) jar sliced mushrooms, drained
- ❖ 4 (6-inch) pita breads, cut in half, forming two pockets.

Preparation:

Heat oil in skillet. Add onion and cook until tender.

Add sandwich steaks and cook until browned.

Pour off fat. Ad soup and mushrooms and heat through. Spoon meat mixture into pita pockets. Serves 4.

Cheesteak Po'Boy

Ingredients:

- ❖ 6 super-thin slices beef
- ❖ 2 teaspoons oil
- ❖ Salt and pepper
- ❖ French loaf, split
- ❖ 3 slices mozzarella cheese
- ❖ 1 cup very thinly-sliced onions

Preparation:

Preheat oven to 350 degrees F.

In a very hot skillet sear beef in 1 teaspoon of oil, about 30 seconds per side, or until just browned. Season with salt and black pepper.

Stuff meat into open bread loaf. Top with cheese and bake until bread is slightly crispy and cheese is melted.

Meanwhile, heat remaining oil in the same skillet and sauté onions until tender.

When sandwich is ready, top sandwich with onions.
Serve with potato chips. Yields 1 sandwich.

Cherry Chicken Salad Sandwich

Ingredients:

- ❖ 2 cups cubed cooked chicken
- ❖ 1/2 cup dried tart cherries
- ❖ 3 green onions, sliced
- ❖ 1/2 cup mayonnaise
- ❖ 1/4 cup plain yogurt
- ❖ 1 tablespoon lemon juice
- ❖ Freshly ground black pepper, to taste
- ❖ Lettuce leaves
- ❖ Chopped fresh parsley
- ❖ 2 to 4 croissants

Preparation:

Combine chicken, cherries and onions in a large bowl; mix well. In another bowl, combine mayonnaise, yogurt, lemon juice and pepper; pour over chicken mixture.

Mix gently. Refrigerate, covered, 1 to 2 hours.

Spoon chicken salad onto sliced croissants; top with lettuce. Garnish with parsley, if desired.

Makes 2 to 4 servings, depending on size of croissants.

Chicken Cordon Bleu Calzones

Ingredients:

- ❖ 4 boneless, skinless chicken breasts (1 pound)
- ❖ 1 cup sliced, fresh mushrooms
- ❖ 1/2 medium onion, chopped
- ❖ 3 tablespoons cornstarch
- ❖ 1 1/4 cups milk
- ❖ 1 tablespoon fresh basil or 1 teaspoon dried basil
- ❖ 1 teaspoon salt
- ❖ 1/4 teaspoon pepper
- ❖ 1 (17 1/2 ounce) package frozen puff pastry, thawed
- ❖ 8 thin slices deli ham
- ❖ 4 slices Provolone cheese

Preparation:

Place chicken in a greased 2-quart dish, cover with water. Cover and bake at 350 degrees F for 30 minutes or until juices run clear.

Meanwhile in skillet, sauté mushrooms and onion in butter until tender.

Combine cornstarch and milk until smooth, stir into skillet mix. Add basil and seasonings.

Bring to a boil, cook, stir for 2 minutes until thickened. Drain chicken.

Cut pastry sheets in half widthwise. On one side of each half, place a chicken breast, 1/4 cup mushroom mixture, two ham slices and one cheese slice.

Fold pastry over fillings and seal edges.

Place on a greased baking sheet.

Brush tops with milk if desired. Bake at 400 degrees for 15-20 minutes or until puffed and golden.

Serves 4.

Chicken Crescents

Ingredients:

- ❖ 3 ounces cream cheese
- ❖ 1 to 2 large cans chicken
- ❖ 1/2 teaspoon salt
- ❖ 1/8 teaspoon pepper
- ❖ 2 tablespoons milk
- ❖ 1 tablespoon chopped onion
- ❖ 2 tablespoons butter, softened
- ❖ 1/2 cup crushed croutons
- ❖ 2 tablespoons melted butter

Preparation:

Cream butter and cream cheese with milk, salt, and pepper. Blend in the chicken.

Open crescent package, and create four rectangles with the crescents, do not tear them into triangles.

Place ¼ of chicken mixture in center of each rectangle.

Pull the corners up around the chicken and seal. Brush with butter, and top with crushed croutons. Bake 20 minutes at 350 degrees F.

Chicago Hot Dogs

Ingredients:

- ❖ All-beef hot dogs
- ❖ Green sweet bell pepper, diced
- ❖ Yellow onions, diced
- ❖ Mustard
- ❖ Sweet pickle relish
- ❖ Dill pickle chips
- ❖ Cucumbers, sliced thin
- ❖ Iceberg lettuce, shredded
- ❖ Tomatoes, diced
- ❖ Hot peppers (pepperoncini)
- ❖ Celery salt

Preparation:

Steam hot dogs and put condiments on table.

Serve on poppy seed buns, if they are available.

NEVER USE CATSUP! Celery salt is a MUST!

CPSIA information can be obtained
at www.ICGtesting.com
Printed in the USA
BVHW061618020321
601493BV00002B/149